OXFORD

English

An International Approach

Exam Workbook

for IGCSE English as a Second Language

4

Chris Akhurst

Money

Comprehension

▶ Read the passage from *The Legend of King Midas* retold by Rachel Redford below and then answer the questions that follow it.

Long ago there lived a king called Midas. In return for some kindness he showed to a stranger, the gods granted him one wish. Midas thought hard and then greedily wished for everything he touched to turn to gold. His wish was granted … with disastrous results.

He ran round the palace chamber like an excited spaniel, touching the ornamental pillars, the chairs with their tapestry covers, the delicately carved cupboards, the stone walls … All were turned to solid gold. In wild excitement, he called to his servants to bring him a feast. He would eat on gold plates just as he had always dreamed of doing! The servants brought him roast swan, chicken in a creamy sauce sprinkled with cinnamon and herbs, fruits, cheese, and a goblet of refreshing juice. Midas suddenly realized after all his running about that he was ravenously hungry. He put out his hand and took up the choicest morsel of chicken dripping with delicious sauce and lifted it to his mouth. But immediately it was hard, inedible gold. He took up the tempting goblet, but it likewise turned to gold. Midas started to feel afraid as he realized the enormity of what he had wished for. Suddenly, his youngest son ran into the chamber.

'Father, Father, what has happened to our home? Why is everything gold?' he cried, and threw himself into his father's arms.

In moments, King Midas was holding a gold statue of his beloved son. 'What have I done? Oh, what have I done?' he cried.

1 Name two pieces of furniture that Midas turned to gold.

....

....

....

2 Why does Midas ask his servants to bring him a feast? Give two reasons.

....

....

....

3 What happened when Midas tried to eat and drink?

....

....

....

4 Is Midas's son pleased to see everything gold? Give one reason for your answer.

....

....

....

....

....

....

5 In your own words, explain what happens to make Midas exclaim, 'Oh, what have I done?'

....

....

....

....

....

Comprehension

▶ Read the following extract from *Dombey and Son* by Charles Dickens and answer the questions that follow.

'Papa! what's money?'

The abrupt question had such immediate reference to the subject of Mr Dombey's thoughts, that Mr. Dombey was quite disconcerted.

'What is money, Paul?' he answered. 'Money?'

'Yes,' said the child, laying his hands on the elbows of his little chair and turning the old face up towards Mr Dombey's, 'what is money?'

Mr Dombey was in a difficulty. He would have liked to give him some explanation involving the terms circulating medium, currency, depreciation of currency, paper, bullion, rates of exchange, value of precious metals in the market, and so forth; but looking down at the little chair, and seeing what a long way down it was he answered: 'Gold, and silver, and copper. Guineas, shillings, half-pence. You know what they are?'
'Oh yes, I know what they are,' said Paul. 'I don't mean that, Papa, I mean what's money after all?'

Heaven and Earth. How old his face was as he turned it up again towards his father's! "What is money after all!" said Mr Dombey, backing his chair a little, that he might the better gaze in sheer amazement at the presumptuous atom that propounded such an inquiry.

1 What is Mr Dombey thinking about at the beginning of this extract?

. . . .

2 What does Mr Dombey want to say money is?
Give two examples.

. . . .

. . . .

3 What does he actually say money is? He mentions six things altogether. Can you pair them up?

. . . .

. . . .

. . . .

4 'What is money after all?' How does this differ from the original question? Say in your own words what you understand Paul to be asking his father.

. . . .

. . . .

. . . .

. . . .

. . . .

. . . .

. . . .

5 How would you answer Paul's question?

. . . .

. . . .

. . . .

. . . .

. . . .

. . . .

Note-making

There was a woman who was beautiful, who started with all the advantages, but who had no luck. She married for love, and the love turned to dust. She had lovely children, but she felt that they had been forced on her, and she could not love them. They looked at her coldly, as if they were finding fault with her, and she felt that she must cover up some fault in herself. But she never knew what she must cover up. But when her children were present, she always felt the centre of her heart go hard. This troubled her, and in her manner she was more gentle and anxious for her children, as if she loved them very much. Only she herself knew that at the centre of her heart was a hard little place that could not feel love, no, not for anybody. Everybody else always said of her, 'She is such a good mother. She loves her children.' Only she herself, and her children themselves, knew that it was not true. They read it in each other's eyes.

There were a boy and two little girls. They lived in a pleasant house, with a garden, and they had servants, and they felt themselves to be better than anyone in the neighbourhood.

Although they lived like rich people, they felt an anxiety in the house. There was never enough money. The mother had a small income, and the father had a small income, but it was not nearly enough for the social position which they had to keep up. The father went into town to some office. But though he had good hopes of a better position, those hopes were never realized. There was never enough money, but the way of life was always kept up.

▶ You have been asked to investigate this family to find out what underlying problems there are. Read the above extract from *The Rocking Horse Winner* by D.H. Lawrence carefully and make notes under each of the following headings.

The woman's relationship with her children

- ....

- ....

What the children thought

- ....

- ....

How the family lived

- ....

- ....

Summary

▶ Using the notes you made about the woman and her family, write a report of not more than 50 words.

Family xxxx – my findings

Informal writing: Money to spend!

Your local newspaper is running a competition offering £1,000 for the most original and interesting description of how the prize money might be spent.

> # COMPETITION
>
> What would you do with £1,000?
> £1,000 to spend on yourself
> Tell us how you would spend £1,000 and the money could be yours!
>
> **Would you**
> ☞ go on a special holiday?
> ☞ put it towards your favourite sport or hobby?
> ☞ or something else?
>
> ✳✳✳✳✳✳✳✳✳✳✳✳✳✳✳✳✳✳✳✳✳✳✳✳✳✳✳✳
>
> *You decide.*
> **In 150–200 words say how would spend the money and why.**
>
> ✳✳✳✳✳✳✳✳✳✳✳✳✳✳✳✳✳✳✳✳✳✳✳✳✳✳✳✳

▶ Write your entry for this competition.

Your article should include:

- details of your choice
- why you have made that choice (rather than another)
- how the money might be allocated
- why your entry should be considered.

Tips

Try to think from the competition judges' point of view.

- *What will they be looking for?*
- *What will impress them?*
- *What will make your entry different from everyone else's?*

Avoid simply sounding self-indulgent.

- *How can you involve other people?*
- *Are you going to put it all towards one thing?*
- *Or might you divide it among a number of options?*

Formal Writing

'Money is power.'

'Money isn't everything.'

'Money makes a man.'

'Money can't buy me love.'

No one wants to be poor but all are aware of the dangers of being rich. What advice would you give?

▶ Write an article on the subject for your school or college magazine.

Tips

How do you make a subject like this interesting?

- *Remember who you are writing for – people of your own age and background.*
- *Be topical – mention things that your readers will recognise and understand.*
- *Think of particular examples – from your own experience perhaps.*

Comprehension

▶ Read this extract from *Cider with Rosie* by Laurie Lee and answer the questions that follow.

The village school at that time provided all the instruction we were likely to ask for. It was a small stone barn divided by a wooden partition into two rooms – The Infants and The Big Ones. There was one dame teacher, and perhaps a young girl assistant. Every child in the valley, crowding there, remained until he was fourteen years old, then was presented to the working field or factory with nothing in his head more troublesome than a jumbled list of wars, and a dreamy image of the world's geography.

The morning came, without any warning, when my sisters surrounded me, wrapped me in scarves, tied up my bootlaces, thrust a cap on my head, and stuffed a baked potato in my pocket.

'What's this?' I said.

'You're starting school, today.'

'I ain't I'm stopping home.'

'Now, come on, Loll. You're a big boy now.'

'I ain't.'

'You are!'

'Boo-hoo.'

They picked me up bodily, kicking and bawling, and carried me up the road.

1 How many classrooms were there in the village school?

. . . .

2 Who did the teaching?

. . . .

3 What two subjects are referred to as being taught there?

. . . .

. . . .

4 Where was it assumed school leavers would go to work?

....

....

5 What did Laurie Lee's sisters call him?

....

6 How did Laurie Lee's sisters prepare him for school?

....

....

....

7 List **four** things that the writer mentions that give the impression that the education provided at the village school was not very advanced.

....

....

....

....

....

Comprehension

▶ Read the following extract from the news report 'Baghdad residents see snow for the first time', Fox News, January 11, 2008 Baghdad, Iraq, and answer the questions that follow.

"For the first time in my life I saw a snow-rain like this falling in Baghdad," said 63-year-old Mohammed Abdul-Hussein. "When I was young, I heard from my father that such rain had fallen in the early '40s on the outskirts of northern Baghdad, but snow falling in Baghdad in such a magnificent scene was beyond my imagination."

After weathering nearly five years of war, Baghdad residents thought they'd pretty much seen it all. But as muezzins were calling the faithful to prayer, the people here awoke to something new.

Snow is common in the mountainous Kurdish areas of northern Iraq, but residents of the capital and surrounding areas could remember just hail. And that only very occasionally. Summer temperatures in Baghdad are routinely a sweltering 120 degrees and winters generally mild.

But this week has been unusually cold and blustery, with overnight temperatures more than 10 degrees below normal. On Thursday morning, the thermometer hovered around freezing after a low of 27, and the Baghdad airport closed because of low visibility.

"I asked my mother, who is 80, whether she'd ever seen snow in Iraq before, and her answer was 'no,'" said Fawzi Karim, a 40-year-old father of five who runs a small restaurant in a village six miles southeast of Baghdad. "This is so unusual, and I don't know whether or not it's a lesson from God."

Talib Haider, a 19-year-old college student, said, "A friend of mine called me at 8 a.m. to wake me up and tell me that the sky is raining snow. I rushed quickly to the balcony to see a very beautiful scene," he said. "I tried to film it with my cell phone camera. This scene has really brought me joy. I called my other friends and the morning turned out to be a very happy one in my life."

An Iraqi who works for The Associated Press said he woke his wife and children shortly after 7 a.m. to "have a look at this strange thing." He then called his brother and sister and found them awake, also watching the "cotton-like snow drops covering the trees."

1 What was the magnificent scene that was in Baghdad?

. . . .

2 Approximately how many years had it been since snow had last fallen in Baghdad?

....

....

3 What was the nearest weather condition to snow that the people of Baghdad could remember?

....

....

....

4 According to the writer why had the snow caused the closure of Baghdad airport?

....

....

5 How did the residents of Baghdad show their excitement at the sight of snow? **Give three details.**

....

....

....

....

....

....

Note-making

You will need the student book for this exercise.

Read the extract from *The Arrangers of Marriage* on pages 36–8 in the student book.

What does Chinaza find strange about her first morning in New York compared to her life in Nigeria?

▶ Under the heading **New York** list the things that she notices.

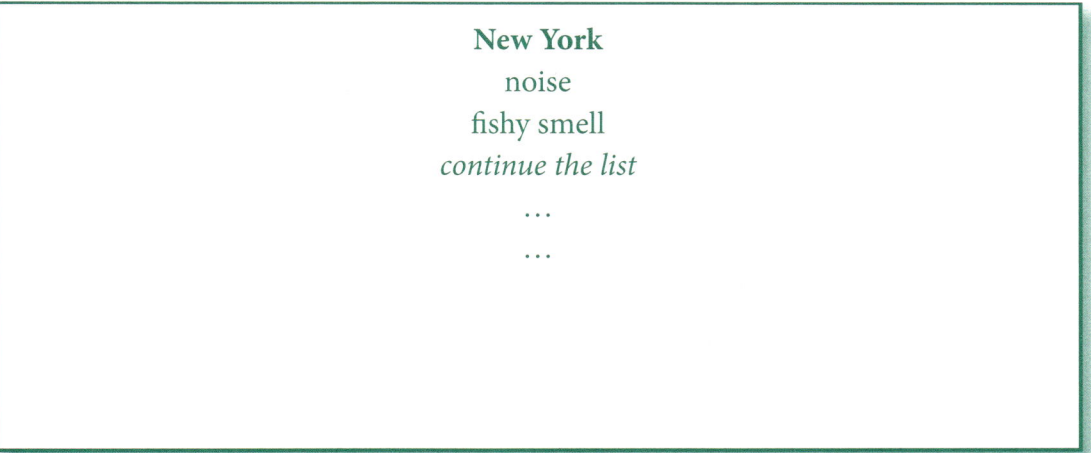

New York
noise
fishy smell
continue the list
…
…

▶ Now do the same for Nigeria.

Summary

▶ Using your notes from the note-making exercise, imagine you are Chinaza and write two paragraphs, one *My first impressions of New York*, and the other *What I miss from Nigeria*.

My first impressions of New York

What I miss from Nigeria

Informal writing

▶ Write an account of an occasion when you were caught in unusual weather conditions – a blizzard, or a heavy rainstorm, perhaps.

Your composition should include:

- a description of the weather
- what is 'unusual' about it
- what you were doing
- how you felt at the time.

Formal writing: a survey

'Schooldays are the happiest of your life.'

You have been asked to write an article on this subject for your school or college magazine.

▶ In preparation for this, conduct a survey of your friends and/or classmates. Then write about your findings.

3 Fire

Comprehension

▶ Read the following extract from *Roughing it in the Bush* by Susanna Moodie and answer the questions that follow.

Before I had the least idea of my danger, I was aroused from the completion of my task by the crackling and roaring of a large fire, and a suffocating smell of burning soot. I looked up at the kitchen cooking-stove. All was right there. I knew I had left no fire in the parlour stove; but not being able to account for the smoke and smell of burning, I opened the door, and to my dismay found the stove red hot, from the front plate to the topmost pipe that let out the smoke through the roof.

My first impulse was to plunge a blanket, snatched from the servant's bed which stood in the kitchen, into cold water. This I thrust into the stove, and upon it I threw water, until all was cool below. I then ran up to the loft, and by exhausting all the water in the house, even to that contained in the boilers upon the fire, contrived to cool down the pipes which passed through the loft. I then sent the girl out of doors to look at the roof, which, as a very deep fall of snow had taken place the day before, I hoped would be completely covered, and safe from all danger of fire.

She quickly returned, stamping and tearing her hair, and making a variety of uncouth outcries, from which I gathered that the roof was in flames.

This was terrible news, with my husband absent, no man in the house, and a mile and a quarter from any other habitation. I ran out to ascertain the extent of the misfortune, and found a large fire burning on the roof between the two stone pipes. The heat of the fires had melted off all the snow, and a spark from the burning pipe had already ignited the shingles. A ladder, which for several months had stood against the house, had been moved two days before to the barn, which was at the top of the hill, near the road; there was no reaching the fire through that source. I got out the dining-table, and tried to throw water upon the roof by standing on a chair placed upon it, but I only expended the little water that remained in the boiler, without reaching the fire. The girl still continued weeping and lamenting.

'You must go for help,' I said.

1 What alerted Susanna to the danger?

. . . .

. . . .

2 What two things did Susanna do to try and cool the red hot stove?

....

....

3 What did Susanna hope would have prevented the cabin roof from catching fire?

....

....

4 How exactly does the servant girl indicate that the roof is in fact in flames?

....

....

5 What two pieces of information are we given that tell us that the fire was indeed terrible news for Susanna?

....

....

6 What does Susanna use to try and reach the fire on the roof?

....

....

7 Write two sentences, one in which you say how you think the fire started, and one giving the message that the servant girl is to take to neighbours.
Make sure that your sentences are accurate and correctly punctuated.

....

....

....

Comprehension

▶ Read this extract from *The Phoenix and the Carpet* by E. Nesbit and answer the questions that follow.

'Oh, stop.' cried Anthea. 'Look at it! Look! look! look! I do believe something is going to happen!'

For the egg was now red-hot, and inside it something was moving. Next moment there was a soft cracking sound; the egg burst in two, and out of it came a flame-coloured bird. It rested a moment among the flames and, as it rested there, the four children could see it growing bigger and bigger under their eyes.

Every mouth was a-gape, every eye a-goggle.

The bird rose in its nest of fire, stretched its wings, and flew out into the room. It flew round and round, and round again, and where it passed the air was warm. Then it perched on the fender. The children looked at each other. Then Cyril put out a hand towards the bird. It put its head on one side and looked up at him, as you may have seen a parrot do when it is just going to speak, so that the children were hardly astonished at all when it said, 'Be careful; I am not nearly cool yet.'

They looked at the bird, and it was certainly worth looking at. Its feathers were like gold. It was about as large as a bantam, only its beak was not at all bantam-shaped. 'I believe I know what it is,' said Robert. 'I've seen a picture.'

'Which of you,' the bird was saying, 'put the egg into the fire?'

'He did,' said three voices, and three fingers pointed at Robert.

The bird bowed; at least it was more like that than anything else.

'I am your grateful debtor,' it said with a high-bred air.

The children were all choking with wonder and curiosity—all except Robert.

He said, 'I know who you are. You are the Phoenix,'

The bird was quite pleased. 'My fame has lived then for two thousand years,' it said.

1 What makes the children think that something is about to happen?

. . . .

. . . .

. . . .

2 What **four** things does the bird do between leaving its egg and taking its first flight?

· ·

· ·

3 Explain in your own words why the children were not surprised that the bird spoke to them.

· ·

· ·

· ·

4 How is Robert able to identify the bird as a phoenix?

· ·

· ·

· ·

5 In your own words as far as possible write a brief description of the phoenix.

· ·

· ·

· ·

· ·

· ·

Information transfer

Josef Simebula is fifteen and a student at St Mary's High School, Manzini, Swaziland. Just recently, his school has been visited by the National Fire and Emergency Service. In addition to showing a film of a fire crew at work, there was an opportunity for students to take part in a training exercise alongside the visiting professional team. He had especially appreciated the chance to learn about the benefits of computer technology in contemporary fire fighting and had been excited when able to listen in as, while they were at his school, the team was called to be on standby for a real-life emergency at the nearby Matsapha airport.

Two years ago, his family home at 21 Magnolia Drive, Manzini, had been badly damaged in a fire that he and his two sisters had been rescued from in the nick of time. After eighteen months of staying with relatives in and around Manzini, they had at last returned to Magnolia Drive, glad to be back after all the upheaval the fire had caused. Fire, he had learned from bitter experience, was a dangerous enemy, and he would be forever grateful for those who had saved his life.

So when the visiting fire team called for young volunteers to join the National Fire Service Cadet Force, Josef was immediately interested, especially when the training officer mentioned that they were recruiting for their summer camp, to be held just after Christmas on the famous Mkhaya Game Reserve.

Eagerly, he took an application form for the camp and completed all he could, confident that his father would give his consent and fill in the section marked 'for parents'.

▶ Imagine that you are Josef. Fill in the form on page 22, using the information above.

SWAZILAND NATIONAL FIRE & EMERGENCY SERVICE CADET FORCE

Cadet camp application form

Date: ....

Name: .... M / F (delete as appropriate) Age: ....

Address: ....

....

School attended: ....

Camp you wish to be considered for: (please tick)

Junior weekend 7-8 Aug (Mbabane) ☐

October event 26-30 Oct (Nelspruit SA) ☐

Summer jamboree 27-31 Dec (Mkhaya) ☐

Have you been on any previous SNFESCF camps? Yes / No

If yes please give details: ....

How did you first hear about the camps? ....

....

Why are you interested in the Fire Service Cadets? (please give all relevant information)

....

....

....

....

....

FOR PARENTS (please read the attached terms and conditions)

'I have read the terms and conditions and give my consent to my son/daughter being considered for the above.'

Signed: .... Full name: ....

Address if different from above: ....

....

Contact details: Telephone: .... E mail: ....

Note-making

▶ Read this extract from *Ash Road* by Ivan Southall.

Three boys, Wallace, Graham and Harry, are camping in the Australian bush. Graham has woken in the early hours of the morning and is boiling water to make some tea.

'Stinkin' hot, isn't it?'

'You can say that again. But this water's awful slow coming to the boil.'

'The wind, I suppose.'

'It's taken two lots of metho already,' said Graham. 'Have you got the lid on?'

'Can't see when it boils if you've got the lid on.'

'Put the lid on, I reckon, or it'll never boil.'

'Don't know where the lid is, do you?'

'Feel for it. It's there somewhere. Use your torch.'

'The battery's flat. Blooming thing. Must have been a crook battery. Hardly used it at all. Now look what I've done! There's the metho bottle knocked for six.'

'You dope,' cried Wallace. 'Pick it up quick. Or we'll lose it all.'

'The cork's in it.' Graham groped for it, feeling a bit of a fool, and said, 'Crumbs.'

'Now what?'

'The cork's not in it, that's what. It must have come out.'

'How could it come out? Honest to goodness …'

'It's burning!' howled Graham.

A blue flame snaked from the little heater up through the rocks towards the bottle in the boy's hand; or at least that was how it seemed to happen. It happened so swiftly it may have deceived the eye. Instinctively, to protect himself, Graham threw the bottle away. There was a shower of fire from its neck, as from the nozzle of a hose.

'Oh, my gosh!' yelled Wallace and tore off his sleeping bag.

'Harry!' he screamed. 'Wake up, Harry!'

They tried to stamp on the fire, but their feet were bare and they couldn't find their shoes. They tried to smother it with their sleeping bags, but it seemed to be everywhere. Harry couldn't even escape from his bag; he couldn't find the zip fastener, and for a few awful moments in his confusion between sleep and wakefulness he thought he was in his bed at home and the house had burst into flames around him. He couldn't come to grips with the situation; he knew only dismay and the wildest kind of alarm. Graham and Wallace, panicking, were throwing themselves from place to place, almost sobbing, beating futilely at a widening arc of fire. Every desperate blow they made seemed to fan the fire, to scatter it farther, to feed it.

'Put it out!' shouted Graham. 'Put it out!'

It wasn't dark any longer. It was a flickering world of tree trunks and twisted boughs, of scrub and saplings and stones, of shouts and wind and smoke and frantic fear. It was so quick. It was terrible.

'Put it out!' cried Graham, and Harry fought out of his sleeping bag, knowing somehow that they'd never get it out by beating at it, that they'd have to get water up from the creek. But all they had was a four-pint billy-can.

▶ You are the first police patrol officer on the scene. Using the extract as your information source, write down your notes under the following headings.

Time and weather conditions

- Dark
- ....
- ....

Graham's account of how the fire started

- Boiling water for tea
- Knocked over metho bottle
- ....
- ....

Wallace's account of waking Harry

- Harry fast asleep
- ....
- ....

Summary

▶ Using your notes and writing as the police officer, write a paragraph reporting how the fire started.

....

....

....

....

....

....

Informal writing: *Rescued!*

Have you ever been involved in a dramatic rescue – from a fire perhaps?

You are staying with friends in a quiet village in a remote part of your country. After a busy day exploring you have enjoyed a lively evening chatting about what you have seen. Tired out, you retire to bed and are quickly asleep. The next thing you know is that you are awoken by the roar of flames …

▶ Write an imaginative account of how you were rescued.

Remember to include:

- a description of the danger you were in – think about the vocabulary you might use to create a picture of the fire
- how you react to the danger – disbelief … growing awareness of danger … panic
- how you attempt to escape
- the moment of rescue
- your sense of relief.

Formal writing

You have accidentally broken a favourite piece of china – a mug or a plate, perhaps.

The piece is at least twenty years old and no longer available in the shops.

▶ Write a letter to the manufacturer explaining exactly what the piece is – its shape and pattern, whether it is part of a set and so on – and asking if they might be able to supply a replacement.

Your letter should include:

- a brief account of what happened
- why you are contacting them
- details of the item you wish to replace
- why the piece is of value to you.

Dear Sir/Madam,

Yours faithfully,

· ·

4 Reaching out

Comprehension

▶ Read the following extract from 'For Venezuela's Poor, Music Opens Doors' by Indira A.R. Lakshmanan and answer the questions that follow.

By the time Lennar Acosta was introduced to classical music at age 15, he had been arrested nine times for armed robbery and drug offenses. A year into the youth's sentence at a state home, a music teacher came to offer the delinquent, abused, and abandoned children there free instruments, instruction, and an opening to a new life.

"Before, nobody trusted me, everyone was afraid of me. I was a discarded kid. The teacher was the first person who understood me and had confidence in me," said Acosta, now 23. Bearing scars on his face from knife attacks during a childhood on the streets, he now knows Beethoven, Tchaikovsky, and Mahler pieces by heart, and long ago cut ties with the criminal gang that raised him.

One of nearly 400,000 children who have passed through Venezuela's state-funded classical music program since it was founded 30 years ago, Acosta says he owes his life to its caring, dedicated teachers – most of whom are graduates of the program.

Today, he plays in the Caracas Youth Orchestra, studies at the national Simón Bolívar Conservatory, and is paid to teach younger clarinetists. He's even mentoring two young men released from his former state home, who are living with him until they get on their feet. "This program opened an unimaginably big door for me. It gives you everything, from instruments to affection, which for me was the most important. Everyone deserves the opportunity they gave us," said Acosta, a crooked smile lighting his face.

1 Who introduced Acosta to classical music?

. . . .

2 What were the children at the state home offered in addition to free instruments? Name **two** things.

. . . .

. . . .

3 How long has Acosta been learning music?

. . . .

4 What instrument does Acosta play?

. . . .

5 How does Acosta now spend his time?
Mention **four** things.

. . . .

. . . .

. . . .

. . . .

. . . .

. . . .

. . . .

6 Write two sentences, one describing Acosta as he was aged 15 and one as he is now
Before:

. . . .

. . . .

. . . .

After:

. . . .

. . . .

Comprehension

▶ Read the story *The Monkey Who Would Be King* by Anthony Horowitz and answer the questions that follow.

Now the august personage of Jade, who was the proper ruler of Heaven, was at his wits' end. So in despair he sent for the one being who was more powerful than him – more powerful in fact, than anyone or anything in the universe: the Buddha.

And so the Buddha came and asked the monkey what all the fuss was about.

'I want to be King of Heaven,' the monkey told him.

'Do you think you are ready for such a position?' the Buddha asked, with a gentle sigh.

'Of course I am,' the monkey snapped. 'I'm ready for anything. Did you know, for example, that I can change myself into seventy-two different shapes? And that I can jump 36,000 miles with one bound? I bet you can't jump that far.'

'You think yourself more powerful than me?' the Buddha asked.

'I most certainly do.'

'Let us see, then, my little friend. Show me how far you can jump. But to prove that you really go as far as you say, write your name on the ground when you get there.'

So the monkey took a deep breath, crouched down and with all his strength leaped into the air. It was a fantastic jump. He soared up into the sky, broke through the clouds and continued into outer space, past the planets, right out of the solar system and beyond the stars. At last he landed in the middle of a great desert where two huge trenches met in the

ground in front of him. Nothing grew for thousands of miles in any direction, but he could see that the ground was laced with a network of lines; making intricate patterns as they crossed over one another. The monkey had no idea where he was, but he was terrifically pleased with himself. He signed his name on the ground with a great flourish and jumped all the way back again.

'Not bad,' the Buddha said. 'But I'm sure you can do even better than that. Why not try again? And this time put all your strength into it.'

'All right,' the monkey said.

He puffed himself up so much that he looked more like a frog than a monkey. Then he scrunched himself into a ball and finally catapulted himself off the ground with legs like rockets. This time he shot through the universe so quickly that he was just a blur. Not only did he break out of the solar system, but he passed the five red pillars which mark the boundary of the created world. At last he landed, this time on the edge of a perfectly circular cliff. A white precipice jutted out just below the ground on which he stood and beneath that all was darkness. The height almost made him dizzy, but he still signed his name as he had been told before jumping all the way back.

'There you are!' he said to the Buddha, unable to stop himself sneering. 'I have proved that I am more powerful even than you. Could you have jumped that far? Of course not! Only the monkey could do it!'

'Wretched creature!' the Buddha cried, getting angry for the first time. He stretched out his hand. 'See here – the full extent of your vanity. You have signed your name twice on my right hand. The first time you landed on my palm, between my life line and my line of destiny.

The second time you reached as far as the tip of my index finger and stood above my nail. Look where you have made your mark. It is the evidence of your own limitations!'

Now the monkey was afraid and began to tremble. He opened his mouth to speak, but it was too late for words. The Buddha seized the wretched creature and shut him up in a magic mountain. And there he remained until the day that he forgot his ambitions and realized that although a monkey can rule the world, only the Buddha is fit to rule the kingdom of Heaven.

1 Why does Jade send for the Buddha?

....

....

2 What evidence does the monkey give to support his claim to be made King of Heaven?
Give **two** details.

....

....

....

3 When the monkey shows how far he can jump, what proof does the Buddha ask for to show that the monkey really jumps as far as he claims?

....

4 Where do the monkey's jumps appear to take him?

First jump: ....

Second jump: ....

5 Where do they actually take him?

First jump: ....

Second jump: ....

6 What does the monkey think he has proved?

....

....

....

....

7 What does the Buddha show he has actually proved?

....

....

....

....

Information transfer

Alejandra Salcedo lives at Calle 30, San Pablo, on the outskirts of Medellin, Colombia. Her email address is alesalcedo@freebee.com. She has been learning the oboe since she was eleven and plays in the orchestra at her school, the Christopher Colombus Institute, Apartado Aereo 77520, Medellin. Her tutor for the oboe, Tjebbe Donner, is very pleased with her progress and has recommended that, to give her more experience of playing with others, she attends a Junior Wind Band Summer School held every summer in Bogotá. He considers that she would benefit from the intermediate course. Alejandra's parents, Carlos and Laura Salcedo, have suggested that, at fourteen, she is a little young to be spending a whole month away from home but are nevertheless willing for her to go, provided she can return to Medellin at weekends. Dr Donner has suggested she apply for a special scholarship and subsistence allowance, as he knows that her family struggles to afford extras for Alejandra and her four siblings. He has also assured them that students on the course are carefully supervised.

▶ Imagine that you are Alejandra. Fill in the application form, using the information above.

JUNIOR WIND BAND SUMMER SCHOOL – APPLICATION FORM

Surname: ………………………………… First name: ……………………………………………

Age: ………………..………………………..……… E mail address: …..……………………………………

Address: ………………………………………………………………..………......………..………………

TO BE COMPLETED IF APPLICANT IS UNDER SIXTEEN:

Parents' names: ……………………………………………………..…….....………..……..…...

Contact details: (if different from above) …………………………………………………….…

………………………………………………………………………………………………………

………………………………………………………………………………………………………

School attended: …………………………………………………………………………………..

Address: …………………………………………………………………………………………….

………………………………………………………………………………………………………

Instrument(s) played: …………………………………………………………………………….

I wish to apply for: (please tick)

Junior Wind Band 1 (advanced)   24th May to 21st June   ☐

Junior Wind Band 2 (intermediate)   21st June to 19th July   ☐

Junior Wind Band (beginners)   19th July to 16th August   ☐

I shall require accommodation: (please circle)

Full four weeks   Mon-Fri only   daytime only

I wish to be considered for: (please circle all applicable)

beginner's bursary   intermediate scholarship   advanced scholarship
day pass (for non-residents)   subsistence allowance

Signed: …………………………………………………………… (parent/guardian if under 16)

Note-making

'Do you know a motto for reaching the stars?'

'Per ardua ad astra' (to the stars through hard work) and 'per aspera ad astra' (to the stars through difficulties) are two Latin tags, or sayings, which have been adopted as mottos for institutions of all kinds right across the world, from Europe and Asia to the USA, Canada, Australia and South America.

The words are intended to encourage people to work hard and struggle to achieve their ambitions: to 'reach for the stars', or to 'reach for the sky'.

The members of *El Sistema*, the Venezuelan youth orchestra, illustrate the spirit of these tags. They have 'reached for the stars' – and succeeded.

José Antonio Abreu, the Venezuelan philanthropist and musician, has devoted his life to reaching out to children from very poor areas of the capital city, Caracas, through enabling them to learn to play musical instruments. He founded *El Sistema*, the National System of Venezuelan Youth and Children's Orchestras, originally called 'Social Action for Music' in 1975. It is now a nationwide organization of 102 youth orchestras, 55 children's orchestras and 270 music centres involving 250,000 young musicians.

This is what he says about his aims in creating *El Sistema* in order to reach out to these children through music:

'Since I was a boy I wanted to be a musician and I had all the necessary support to do so. My dream was that under-privileged Venezuelan children should have the same opportunity. Music has to be recognized as an agent of social development in the highest sense, because it transmits the highest values – solidarity, harmony, mutual compassion. It has the ability to unite an entire community and express sublime feelings.'

▶ You are to give a short talk to your class about the Venezuelan youth orchestra *El Sistema*. Using the information on this page, make brief notes as the basis for your talk.

The orchestra

- ....

- ....

The founder

- ....

- ....

Why he founded it

• ....

• ....

Summary

▶ Write a short account of the orchestra and its founder based on your notes. You should aim to write not more than 50 words.

....

....

....

....

....

....

....

....

....

Informal writing: a cautionary tale

The Monkey Who Would Be King is a cautionary tale. It warns us about the folly of boasting, or claiming that we can do things that are actually beyond us. Like the monkey, we can appear very foolish when we what we say doesn't match what we can actually do.

▶ Write a modern cautionary tale to show the folly of someone whose actions cannot match their words.

Tips

Keep your story simple – a boy who boasts to his school friends that he can do something (drive a car or climb a tree, perhaps) with disastrous results.

Think of words that will help contrast what happens and what was supposed to happen (look again at *The Monkey Who Would Be King* for ideas and examples).

Formal writing: a letter

Your school council has held a meeting to discuss better facilities for children and young people in your area. At that meeting all agreed that there is not enough for them to do, especially in the evenings, and that there is a clear link between that and the amount of petty crime and antisocial behaviour in the area.

Suggestions included:

- making school playing fields available at set times for supervised leisure activities
- organizing a monthly disco using the school hall
- developing all-age evening classes for extended learning and the pursuit of hobbies
- establishing a toddler playgroup
- opening a 'drop-in centre' for mothers with young children
- appointing a local Youth Officer to co-ordinate and oversee arrangements.

▶ You have been appointed by your school council to write to your local government representatives about the problem. Using some or all of the above and including ideas of your own, write that letter.

Dear Sir/Madam,

Yours faithfully,

. . . .

Comprehension

▶ Read the following extract from *The Dinosaur Hunters* by Deborah Cadbury and answer the questions that follow.

Mary Anning (1799–1847) lived with her impoverished family in Lyme Regis on the south coast of England in the early nineteenth century. Mary and her brother Joseph collected shells and bones which could be unearthed from the cliffs and sold them as curios to make a little money for the family.

While Joseph, Mary's elder brother, was apprenticed to an upholsterer, Mary continued to search the beach for fossils. One day she found a beautiful ammonite, or snake-stone. As she carried her trophy from the beach, a lady in the street offered to buy it for half a crown. For Mary this was wealth indeed, enough to buy some bread, meat and possibly tea and sugar for a week. From that moment she was 'fully determined to go down upon the beach again'.

During 1811 – the exact date is not known – Joseph made a remarkable discovery while he was walking along the beach. Buried in the shore a strange shape caught his eye. As he unearthed the sand and shale, the giant head of a fossilized creature slowly appeared, four feet long, the jaws filled with sharp interlocking teeth, the eye sockets huge like saucers. On one side of the head the bony eye was entire, staring out at him from some unknown past. The other eye was damaged, deeply embedded in the broken bones of the skull. Joseph immediately hired the help of two men to assist him and uncovered what was thought to be the head of a very large crocodile.

Joseph showed Mary where he had found the enormous skull but since that section of the beach was covered by a mudslide for many months afterwards it was difficult to look for more relics of the creature. Nearly a year elapsed before Mary, who was still scarcely more than twelve or thirteen, came across a fragment of fossil buried nearly two feet deep on the shore, a short distance from where Joseph had found the head.

Working with her hammer around the rock, she found large vertebrae, up to three inches wide. As she uncovered more, it was possible to glimpse ribs buried in the limestone, several still connected to the vertebrae. She gathered some men to help her extract the fossils from the shore. Gradually, they revealed an entire backbone, made up of sixty vertebrae. On one side, the shape of the skeleton could be clearly seen; it was not unlike a huge fish with a long tail. On the other side, the ribs were 'forced down upon the vertebrae and squeezed into a mass' so that the shape was harder to discern. As the fantastic creature emerged from its ancient tomb they could see this had been a giant animal, up to seventeen feet long.

1 Why did Mary decide to keep looking for fossils?

....

....

2 How old was Mary when Joseph made his remarkable discovery?

....

....

3 Why did Joseph think that the giant fossil was the head of a very large crocodile?

....

....

....

4 Why was it nearly a year before the next piece of the fossil was found?

....

....

....

5 Give a brief description in your own words of the remarkable find that Joseph and Mary made.

....

....

....

....

Note-making

▶ Read the following extract from *The Storyteller's Daughter* by Saira Shah.

I am three years old. I am sitting on my father's knee. He is telling me of a magical place: the fairytale landscape you enter in dreams. Fountains fling diamond droplets into mosaic pools. Coloured birds sing in the fruit-laden orchards. The pomegranates burst and their insides are rubies. Fruit is so abundant that even the goats are fed on melons. The water has magical properties: you can fill to bursting with fragrant *pilau*, then step to the brook and drink – and you will be ready to eat another meal. On three sides of the plateau, majestic mountains tower, capped with snow. The fourth side overlooks a sunny valley where, gleaming far below, sprawls a city of villas and minarets. And here is the best part of the story: it is true.

The garden is in Paghman, where my family had its seat for nine hundred years. The jewel-like city it overlooks is the Afghan capital, Kabul. The people of Paghman call the capital Kabul *jan*: beloved Kabul. We call it that too, for this is where we belong. 'Whatever outside appearances may be, no matter who tells you otherwise, this garden, this country, these are your origins. This is where you are truly from. Keep it in your heart, Saira *jan*. Never forget,' says my father.

*

Saira Shah travelled to Afghanistan as an adult in 2001

But I need to know what is fact and what is fairytale more than I need the reassurance of the myth. Only truth can answer the questions that for years I haven't even dared to ask my own heart. Does the Afghanistan of our myths really exist? Are we still Afghans? And if I am not an Afghan, what am I?

There is one last place to visit. As I climb the steep mountainside to the Paghman plateau, I am gripped with fear. If the magical gardens my father told me of never existed, then part of me will be a lie as well. I am standing upon a desolate plateau. No birds sing. The fruit trees have been cut down for firewood. The irrigation channels are bombed and the once-fertile soil is dry. All my life, I have carried a picture of this place in my heart. All my life, this is where I have most longed to be.

The ground is seeded with mines and strewn with the debris of its former splendour: the blue mosaic tiles, the broken watercourses and the dried-out fountains. This myth, at least, was true: in my mind's eye, I can reconstruct what once must have been a magical garden. Sa'adi once gazed on the full bloom of a garden such as this. His poet's vision saw that its beauty would fade. 'The rose of the garden has no continuance,' he said. 'Do not become attached to what will not endure.' He decided to create a garden that time could not destroy. He built his rose garden – his great work, the Gulistan – out of stories. It has survived for eight hundred years. 'Roses,' he said, 'live but for a few days. My Rose Garden will never die.'

Towering above me, unchanging, eternal, are the mountains. Down in the valley, a city of towers and minarets sparkles in the late-afternoon sun. Kabul *jan* – beloved Kabul – lies like a jewel at my feet. I know by now that its beauty is an illusion: close up, the city is in ruins, as shattered and broken as this garden. I have missed the golden age. I have come too late.

My journey here has taken me over twenty years. While I was making my way towards it, the place that inspired the myth has been destroyed. But only because of the myth – the map of tales my family drew for me all those years ago – can I recognize the beauty in this ruin.

Saira Shah

▶ You have been asked to write a short article about the effects of war on an area, using Saira Shah's account of her trip to Afghanistan as an example. To prepare for it, make brief notes under the headings below.

The garden of her father's memories

   the setting

....

....

....

   what is in the garden

....

....

....

The remains of the garden that Saira discovers

   the setting

....

....

....

   what is left of the garden

....

....

....

   what the ruined garden contains

....

....

....

Summary: Before ... and after

▶ Using the notes that you have made, write two paragraphs describing the garden.

When it was Saira's family home

As she found it in 2001

Informal writing

In 1817 the English poet Shelley won a competition to write about a vast ruin of a statue that had been discovered in the Egyptian desert. His winning entry is the famous poem 'Ozymandias'.

Now it is your turn.

▶ Using the picture on page 105 of the student book as your inspiration, write a short story or descriptive piece.

Things to think about:

- Whose statue is it?
- Why did he (she?!) have it set up?
- Was it a great ruler? A god? A conquering soldier?
- How long ago was it?
- What was life like then?

Perhaps your story will be about how the statue came to be broken up.

- What happened?
- Was the conqueror in turn conquered?

Tell your story.

Formal writing: The seven ages of man

In Shakespeare's play *As You Like It*, one of the characters describes life as being divided into seven 'ages' or periods of time: 'first the infant', then the 'schoolboy with his satchel' and so on till the seventh age, 'second childishness'. As you might expect, the seven ages Shakespeare lists are seven stages in life as he saw it in England 400 years ago:

1. baby
2. schoolboy
3. lover
4. soldier

5. justice (judge)
6. retired gentleman
7. extreme old age

How different would your twenty-first century 'seven ages' be from Shakespeare's?

▶ Make a list of your twenty-first century seven ages (male or female, or both – you choose) and then choose one of your ages to describe in detail.

Your description might include:

- **what a typical person of that age might look like (e.g. clothing, hairstyle)**
- **some characteristics typical of that age (e.g. interests, obsessions)**
- **an example or two of what someone that age might be found doing**
- **attitudes associated with that age.**

6 Escaping

Comprehension

▶ Read the following extract from *Descent into the Maelstrom* by Edgar Allan Poe and answer the questions that follow.

In less than a minute the storm was upon us – in less than two the sky was entirely overcast – and what with this and the driving spray, it became suddenly so dark that we could not see each other. Such a hurricane as then blew it is folly to attempt describing. The oldest seaman in Norway never experienced anything like it. At the first puff, both our masts went by the board as if they had been sawn off – the mainmast taking with it my youngest brother, who had lashed himself to it for safety.

Our boat was the lightest feather of a thing that ever sat upon water. It had a flat deck, with only a small hatch near the bow, and this hatch it had always been our custom to batten down when about to cross the Ström, as a precaution. I threw myself flat on deck, with my hands grasping a ringbolt near the foot of the fore-mast.

As I was trying to collect my senses, I felt somebody grasp my arm. It was my elder brother, and my heart leaped for joy, for I thought he had gone overboard – but the next moment all this joy was turned into horror – for he put his mouth close to my ear, and screamed out the word 'Moskoe-ström!'

I knew what he meant by that one word – I knew what he wished to make me understand. With the wind that now drove us on, we were bound for the whirl of the Strom, and nothing could save us! The Moskoe-ström whirlpool was about a quarter of a mile dead ahead. I dragged my pocket watch. It was not going. I glanced at its face by the moonlight, and then flung it into the ocean. It had run down at seven o'clock! We were behind the time of the slack, there was no going back, and the whirl of the Ström was in full fury!

1 What **two** things indicate the onset of the storm?

. . . .

. . . .

2 Explain in your own words what happens to the narrator's younger brother.

. . . .

. . . .

3 From the evidence of this passage what do you understand the sailors' instruction to 'batten down the hatches' to mean?

. . . .

. . . .

4 What **two** reactions does the narrator have to the appearance of his elder brother?

. . . .

. . . .

. . . .

5 Explain how these experienced seamen came to be caught in the whirlpool.

. . . .

. . . .

. . . .

6 Describe briefly in your own words the development of the storm from its first onset to the point where the boat is driven into the whirlpool.

. . . .

. . . .

. . . .

. . . .

. . . .

Note-making

Elephants escaping Zimbabwe damage Zambian crops and property

Michael Durham reports from Zambia, South-East Africa

Hundreds of wild elephants are the latest refugees from violence and disorder in Zimbabwe. The animals are fleeing the country by wading across the Zambezi River to escape being shot or trapped by so-called 'war veterans' and illegal hunters.

Game wardens in Zambia say record numbers of elephants are crossing the Zambezi, which forms the border between the two countries, to avoid being poached by armed gangs in Zimbabwe. 'Elephants are quite intelligent and can communicate. They know they are safer on this side of the river,' said one game warden.

The exodus is an indication of the devastation facing wildlife in Zimbabwe, where animals are said to be at risk of indiscriminate slaughter in reserves and former privately owned game parks. With the breakdown of law and order, animals of all kinds are reportedly being poached on a massive scale for ivory and even for food.

At Mosi-o-Tunya National Park, on the Zambian side of the Zambezi River, elephants are arriving daily from across the river. Wildlife experts say the movement is much larger than the normal seasonal emigration and is causing a serious problem for Zambian authorities. There are so many elephants trapped in a small area that serious damage is being caused to the environment.

About 200 elephants are thought to be living in the small Zambian national park, an area more used to a population of about 50. The elephants are stripping the area of foliage and knocking down trees, there are conflicts between the wild elephants and farmers and two local villagers have been killed by elephants.

The Zambian representative of the David Shepherd Wildlife Foundation, said: 'Lawlessness in Zimbabwe is definitely a factor in driving more elephants into Zambia and causing a problem here. If an elephant is shot, others will leave the area for safety. Elephants can communicate over up to seven miles – and they never forget.'

▶ You have been asked to produce a report on the movement of elephants across the border between Zimbabwe and Zambia. As part of your preparation, make brief notes on Michael Durham's article under the headings provided.

What the elephants are doing

- ....

- ....

Why are they moving in such numbers?

- ....

- ....

- ....

Consequences of this movement

- ....

- ....

- ....

Summary

▶ Now write your report, making use of the notes you have made.

Informal writing: *I alone escaped* ...

You and a friend are alone on a remote beach when a man in an advanced state of exhaustion staggers out of the water and collapses at your feet. Together you pull him to safety and he gradually revives sufficiently to tell you a remarkable story.

▶ What did he say?

Tips

• Take time to think about the setting – how did he suddenly appear? (Are there rocks that might have hidden him, or a headland, perhaps?)
• Begin at the point where the man starts to speak.
• Include breaks – where he breaks off in terror, needs further reviving, is distracted, or … .
• Only tell his story – what happens afterwards is not part of it.

Formal writing

Getting away from it all

Do you ever wish you could escape – get away from your present surroundings to a new existence?

Where would you go?
What would you want to get away from?
What would you be reluctant to leave?

What considerations would you have to think over?
*   effect on others – your family, perhaps
*   the risks involved.

How would you justify it?
Would it just be 'running away' or would it be a once-in-a-lifetime opportunity?

▶ Write an article for your school/college magazine discussing the question.

7 In the dark

Comprehension

▶ Read the entry for 17 August from Mina Harker's journal in this extract from *Dracula* by Bram Stoker. Then answer the questions that follow.

17 August:– No diary for three whole days. I have not had the heart to write. Some sort of shadowy pall seems to be coming over our happiness. Lucy seems to be growing weaker; I do not understand Lucy's fading away as she is doing. She eats well and sleeps well, and enjoys the fresh air, but all the time the roses in her cheeks are fading, and she gets weaker and more languid day by day. At night I hear her gasping as if for air.

I keep the key of our door always fastened to my wrist at night, but she gets up and walks about the room, and sits at the open window. Last night I found her leaning out when I woke up, and when I tried to wake her I could not. She was in a faint. When I managed to restore her, she was weak as water, and cried silently between long, painful struggles for breath. When I asked her how she came to be at the window she shook her head and turned away.

I looked at her throat just now as she lay asleep, and the tiny wounds seem not to have healed. They are still open, and, if anything, larger than before, and the edges of them are faintly white. They are like little white dots with red centres. Unless they heal within a day or two, I shall insist on the doctor seeing about them.

1 Why has Mina not written in her diary for three whole days?

....

....

2 What three things does Mina mention to show that Lucy is living a healthy lifestyle?

....

....

....

....

3 Name two things that suggest that Lucy is in fact far from well.

....

....

....

4 How does Mina try to prevent intruders from harming Lucy?

....

....

....

5 Yet Lucy has been harmed. Explain in your own words in a sentence of between 12 and 20 words what we learn in this extract about the injuries she has received.

....

....

....

6 Imagine that you are the local doctor called in by Mina to examine her friend. Using the evidence of this extract, write your brief report.

....

....

....

....

....

Comprehension

▶ Read the extract from *The Strange Case of Dr Jekyll and Mr Hyde* by R.L. Stevenson and answer the following questions.

A maid servant living alone in a house not far from the river had gone upstairs to bed about eleven. Although a fog rolled over the city in the small hours, the early part of the night was cloudless, and the lane, which the maid's window overlooked, was brilliantly lit by a full moon. As she sat she became aware of an aged and beautiful gentleman with white hair drawing near along the lane; and advancing to meet him, another and very small gentleman, to whom at first she paid less attention. When they had come within speech (which was just under the maid's eyes) the older man bowed and approached the other with a very pretty manner of politeness. It did not seem as if the subject of his address were of great importance; indeed, from his pointing, it sometimes appeared as if he were only inquiring his way; but the moon shone on his face as he spoke, and the girl observed his old-world kindness of disposition. Presently her eye wandered to the other, and she was surprised to recognize in him a certain Mr. Hyde, who had once visited her master, and for whom she had conceived a dislike. He had in his hand a heavy cane, with which he was trifling; but he answered never a word, and seemed to listen with an ill-contained impatience.

1 What was the weather like when the maid servant went to bed?

. . . .

. . . .

. . . .

2 Why is the maid able to see clearly events taking place in the lane?
Give **two** reasons.

. . . .

. . . .

. . . .

. . . .

3 As the two men approach, what does the maid see that makes her think that one is asking for directions from the other?

. . . .

. . . .

. . . .

. . . .

4 How does the other man respond?

. . . .

. . . .

. . . .

. . . .

5 In this extract the author gives us several clues as to the character of these two men. Give **four** reasons for us to believe that the older man is kind and gentle.

. . . .

. . . .

. . . .

. . . .

. . . .

Information transfer / Summary

Sandra Jeavons is a Media Studies student at the University of Dundee, Scotland. On 7th April at about 8 p.m. she was walking back along Perth Road to her digs in 32B Thomson Street, Dundee DD1 4HW after an evening working in the University Library when she disturbed a group of teenagers surrounding an elderly lady. As she approached they ran off in the direction of the railway line and the river, knocking the old lady to the ground in their haste to get away.

Sandra saw that the lady was not seriously hurt. But she was badly shaken up, so the student helped her to a sitting position and gave her a drink of water before calling an ambulance on her mobile phone (07941 705840). While they waited for the ambulance to arrive, the old lady, who was still very frightened and in a state of shock, gasped out her story between choking sobs.

From what Sandra could make out it appeared that the lady, Mary McGilp, had been returning from a visit to a friend nearby when the youths had suddenly rushed up to her. They had taunted her and pushed her against the wall. They had demanded money and were trying to grab her handbag when Sandra had surprised them and they had run off.

When the ambulance arrived, the paramedics confirmed that she had no serious injuries but, in view of her age and frailty decided to take her to hospital. That proved the right decision because in the ambulance Mary suddenly took a turn for the worse. She suffered a heart attack and was unconscious upon arrival at the hospital. Unfortunately, Mary never rallied and died later that night without regaining consciousness.

Sandra had offered to go in the ambulance with her but that help had been declined by Mary, who had insisted that she would be all right. So it was a shocked Sandra who opened her door next morning to find two police officers standing there. DI Marion Crawford and her assistant PC Shona MacFinnan told Sandra the sad news and asked her to complete an incident report form for them.

▶ Imagine you are Sandra and complete the incident report using the above information.

TAYSIDE POLICE

Incident Report

Date: .. / .. / ....   Police in attendance: ....

DETAILS OF INFORMANT

Name: ....

Address: ....

....

Telephone: .... E mail: ....

Occupation: ....

DETAILS OF INCIDENT

Date: .. / .. / ....   Approx. time: ....

Where incident took place: ....

Were you: (please circle)   a victim   a witness   neither

Give in your own words a brief statement of what took place

Only include information you can verify

Give details of your source ['I saw …'; 'X told me ..'etc.]

....

....

....

....

....

....

....

....

Signed: ....

Informal writing: contrasts

Picture a familiar scene – the view from your window, perhaps.

Think how its appearance changes according to the time of day, or night.

▶ Make **two** contrasting lists of words you might use to describe:

- the scene at midday
- that same scene at midnight.

midday	midnight
light	dark
sunlit	black
clear	murky
……	……
……	……
……	……
……	……

▶ Now, with the help of your lists, write **two** paragraphs, describing the contrasting scenes.

What doesn't change?

Do objects appear larger, smaller in the dark?

What are your feelings as you picture the scene?

- Bring out the contrasts
- Don't forget to refer to sounds in your descriptions
- And what about taste, touch and smell?

Formal writing: My Favourite Read

Your local library is holding a competition entitled *My Favourite Read*.

!! Competition !!

Are you a Dracula fan?
Or do you prefer the great outdoors?

Is classical fiction your favourite?
Or maybe – history
Travellers' tales
Science fiction
Tales of magic and mystery
Suspense
Crime
Adventure
Humour

My Favourite Read

Tell us what you enjoy reading and why
in not more than 250 words.

▶ Write your entry for the above competition.

8 Viewpoint

Comprehension

▶ Read this extract from *The Sniper* by Liam O'Flaherty and then answer the questions that follow.

The long June twilight faded into night. Dublin lay enveloped in darkness, but for the dim light of the moon, that shone through fleecy clouds, casting a pale light as of approaching dawn over the streets and the dark waters of the Liffey. Around the beleaguered Four Courts the heavy guns roared. Here and there through the city machine guns and rifles broke the silence of the night, spasmodically, like dogs barking on lone farms. Republicans and Free States were waging civil war.

On a rooftop near O'Connell Bridge, a Republican sniper lay watching. Beside him lay his rifle and over his shoulders were slung a pair of field glasses. His face was the face of a student – thin and ascetic, but his eyes had the cold gleam of the fanatic. They were deep and thoughtful, the eyes of a man who is used to looking at death.

1 This could be any June evening in Dublin, but, as we are told in the final sentence of the opening paragraph, civil war is taking place. How does the sound of war disturb the quiet?
Give two examples.

. . . .

. . . .

2 What word tells us that the noise is not constant?

. . . .

3 Why is the sound of gunfire likened to the barking of farm dogs?
Give two reasons.

. . . .

. . . .

4 What two pieces of equipment does the sniper have?

. . . .

. . . .

5 We are not told the sniper's name but what do we learn about him from this extract?
Mention four things.

. . . .

. . . .

. . . .

. . . .

. . . .

. . . .

. . . .

6 The writer chooses contrasting words to describe war and peace. How many examples can you find?

. . . .

. . . .

. . . .

. . . .

. . . .

Comprehension

▶ Read the passage below and then answer the following questions.

Learning to paint or draw using perspective requires a knowledge of geometry to mimic the viewpoint of the human eye. Painters since the Renaissance have mastered the effects of three dimensions, painted on a two-dimensional surface, to great effect. When this is achieved to a high degree, it creates what is known as a *trompe l'oeil* illusion.

This 1533 painting by the German artist Holbein the Younger, court painter to Henry VIII of England, shows the mastery that had been achieved by the sixteenth-century in making a painting a very convincing stage set. Here the painter masters the effects of the illusion of life to represent the rich court robes and artefacts of learning and discovery of the two ambassadors.

But the viewpoint is more complex than it might at first appear. Why, for instance, does the lute have a broken string? And what is the strange shape that seems to hover in the foreground? Now try viewing the image from the oblique right, as if you were standing to the side of the painting. Only when you view it from this distorted perspective does the perfectly formed image of a skull come into view.

1 What does the writer tell us that artists need to know in order to copy what the eye sees?

. . . .

2 Why are the three dimensions of a painting described as an illusion?

. . . .

. . . .

3 Who are the two men in the painting?

. . . .

4 A close look at the painting reveals a more complex picture than might be seen at first glance. What **two** things does the writer mention?

. . . .

. . . .

5 What comment about riches is the artist making? Give your answer in **one sentence of between 12 and 20 words.**

....

....

....

....

....

....

6 Write a brief description (or word picture) of one of these two men.

....

....

....

....

....

....

....

....

Information transfer

Wolfgang Schneider is seventeen and a student at Innsbruck Arts Academy, where he studies painting and drawing and the History of Art. He lives at 12 Kirchenstrasse, Götzens, Innsbruck 57734 (tel: 896751) and travels to college daily by bus. This is a troublesome journey, especially in the winter months, when the winding road down the mountain can be very treacherous. Sometimes it is impassable and can remain blocked for days.

This interferes with Wolfgang's studies, although he doesn't altogether mind as it enables him to spend more time on his other passion in life – skiing. He has skied since he was six years old and is a part-time junior instructor with his local Ski School. His father, Dieter, once represented Austria in giant slalom skiing and would be keen for Wolfgang to follow in his steps.

But Wolfgang wants above all to be an artist and has set his sights on going to the prestigious Vienna School of Art when his Innsbruck course finishes in a year's time. His mother Margrit's grandfather was the renowned portrait painter Friedrich Hauser and Wolfgang, who bears his famous ancestor's surname as his middle name, wants to live up to that reputation.

First he must do well in his studies and he has applied for a grant from the Innsbruck 'Supporting Young Talent' scheme to enable him to afford lodgings close to the Academy, rather than having to make the daily bus journey.

▶ Imagine you are Wolfgang. Fill in the application form.

Innsbruck 'Supporting Young Talent'

Application for a grant

Full name: ....   Age next birthday: ....

Address: ....

....

Telephone: ....

Parents' names: ....

Place of study: ....

Details of course: ....

....

Leisure interest(s) ....

Give details of any part-time employment: ....

....

....

....

Why are you applying for a 'Supporting Young Talent' grant? (please give details of how the money
will be used):

....

....

....

....

....

Additional information (please include anything relevant to your application – such as proposed
further study, career prospects, aspirations):

....

....

....

Signed: ....

Note-making

You will need the student book for this exercise. Read again the online news article on pages 168–9 about the APOPO project to train rats to detect landmines. Read also **Writing a report** on page 169.

You have been working on the APOPO project in Mozambique and are considering extending your operations into Angola in Africa and have been asked to write a report on your operations with the rats in Mozambique for the Angolan government minister.

▶ Prepare some notes that you would use to write that report.

Make **two** short notes under each heading.

The problem of landmines

- large number of deaths and injuries caused by landmines

- ....

- ....

How rats are employed

- ....

- ....

What the training scheme involves

- ....

- ....

Why they are better than sniffer dogs

- ....

- ....

Summary

▶ Now use your notes as the basis for your report (see page 169 of the student book).

Informal writing

▶ Tell a story in which a minor dispute gradually grows to become a major disagreement, with serious consequences.

Suggestions

- Friends become first rivals, then opponents and finally enemies …
- Neighbours begin by sharing a patch of ground but gradually are more competitive and challenging, destroying one another's efforts and …
- Brothers grow up together but drift apart and dispute with one another …
- A remark intended as a joke is misunderstood …
- Try giving your story an unexpected ending.

Formal writing: Giving your views

▶ Read the piece about the 'Pied Piper of Hamelin' on page 167.

The people of Hamelin were so desperate that when the Pied Piper said that he would get rid of the rats he was offered a great deal of money if he succeeded. However, once he has worked his magic and drowned all the rats in the river, he returns to claim his reward, only to be told that the price has dropped –

> But as for the guilders, what we spoke
> Of them, as you well know, was in joke,
> Beside, our losses have made us thrifty.
> A thousand guilders! Come, take fifty!

In his anger, the Pied Piper exacts a terrible revenge, as you can discover if you read the rest of Robert Browning's poem.

But the question is raised: 'How much do we value the work of those who do difficult or unpleasant jobs for us?'

Rat catchers, snake charmers, and pest controllers often struggle to make a living. Refuse collectors and sewage workers are not very well paid.

Is that right? How do we decide what rewards to give (how much to pay) those who work for us?

What do you think?

▶ Imagine that the refuse collectors in your local town are on strike for better pay and conditions.

Write a letter to your local newspaper EITHER in support of the workers' demands OR complaining about the chaos and confusion that the strike is causing.

Dear Sir/Madam,

Yours faithfully,

. . . .

9 Colour

Comprehension

▶ Read the following extract from *The Story of Colours* by Subcomandante Insurgente Marcos and then answer the questions that follow.

The gods were fighting, because the world was very boring with only two colours to paint it. And their anger was a true anger because only the two colours took their turns with the world: the black which ruled the night and the white which strolled about during the day. And then there was a third which wasn't a real colour. It was the grey which painted the dusks and the dawns so that the black and the white didn't bump into each other so hard. And these gods were quarrelsome but wise. They had a meeting and they finally agreed to make more colours. They wanted to make it more joyous for people – who were blind as bats – to take a walk and take pleasure in their surroundings.

One of the gods took to walking so he could think better. And he thought his thoughts so deeply that he didn't look where he was going. And he tripped on a stone so big that he hit his head and it started to bleed.

And the god, after screaming and squawking for quite a while, looked at his blood and saw that it was a different colour, one that wasn't like the other two colours. And he went running to where the other gods were and showed them the new colour, and they called the colour red, the third colour to be born.

After that, another god looked for a colour to paint the feeling of hope. He found it, though it took him a little while, and he went to show it to the assembly of gods, and they named this colour green, the fourth colour.

Another one started to dig deep into the earth. 'What are you doing?' asked the other gods. 'I'm trying to find the heart of the earth', he answered, throwing dirt all over the place. In time he arrived at the heart of the earth and he showed it to the other gods and they called this fifth colour brown.

1 What were the only two colours that the gods originally had to paint with?

. . . .

. . . .

2 What did the gods use grey for?

. . . .

3 Why did the gods agree to make more colours?
Give two reasons.

....

....

4 How was the third colour discovered?

....

5 List the five colours and where the gods found them.

1............   ....

2............   ....

3............   ....

4............   ....

5............   ....

6 Continue the story as you think it might have described the discovery of another colour, one of your choice.

....

....

....

....

....

....

Informal writing

▶ Write a short story entitled **Red is for Danger**.

You may use the idea of the title in any way you like but the colour must be significant in some way.

Formal writing: speech

An international youth organization is holding a summer camp somewhere near you shortly with delegates attending from all over the world. As the host nation your country has set up a competition to compose a speech welcoming delegates to the camp. The writer of the best speech will represent your country at the camp and get to deliver the speech at the opening ceremony.

▶ Write your entry for the competition.

Tips

Think about the following ideas.

What is bringing the delegates together?

- A better understanding of different cultures
- A chance to meet people of your own age from other parts of the world
- Cross-cultural exchange – music, dancing, sport, leisure.

What features of your country or locality might you mention?

How might you make the delegates feel especially welcome?

What kind of speech do you think will be best?

- Light-hearted – to put everyone at ease
- Passionate – about your country perhaps
- Serious – a call for world peace perhaps.

How will you start?

How will you finish?

Comprehension

▶ Read the following extract from *Txting: the Gr8 Db8* by David Crystal and answer the questions that follow.

People think that the written language seen on mobile phone screens is new and alien, but all the popular beliefs about texting are wrong. Its graphic distinctiveness is not a new phenomenon, nor is its use restricted to the young. There is increasing evidence that it helps rather than hinders literacy. And only a very tiny part of it uses a distinctive orthography. A trillion text messages sent worldwide in 2005 might seem a lot, but when we set these alongside the multi-trillion instances of standard orthography in everyday life, they appear as no more than a few ripples on the surface of the sea of language. Texting has added a new dimension to language use, but its long-term impact is negligible. It is not a disaster.

Although many texters enjoy breaking linguistic rules, they also know they need to be understood. There is no point in paying to send a message if it breaks so many rules that it ceases to be intelligible. When messages are longer, containing more information, the amount of standard orthography increases. Many texters alter just the grammatical words (such as 'you' and 'be'). As older and more conservative language users have begun to text, an even more standardized style has appeared. Some texters refuse to depart at all from traditional orthography. And conventional spelling and punctuation is the norm when institutions send out information messages, as in this university text to students: 'Weather Alert! No classes today due to snow storm', or in the texts which radio listeners are invited to send in to programmes. These institutional messages now form the majority of texts in cyberspace – and several organizations forbid the use of abbreviations, knowing that many readers will not understand them. Bad textiquette.

1 What popular ideas about texting does David Crystal say are mistaken? **Give two examples.**

. . . .

. . . .

. . . .

. . . .

2 How many text messages were sent worldwide in 2005?

....

....

3 Explain in your own words why, according to Crystal, texting is 'not a disaster'.

....

....

....

....

4 What does Crystal maintain is the most important consideration when sending a text?

....

....

....

....

5 Summarise in **one sentence** and in your own words why institutions use conventional spelling and punctuation.

....

....

....

....

Comprehension

▶ Read the following extract from the student book and answer the following questions.

Beowulf [bear-wolf] is the only epic of its time to have survived, and is one of the most important works of European literature, set in the Kingdom of the Geats (Scandinavia), a culture which did not survive beyond the end of the sixth century CE. If the hero, Beowulf, was based on a real man, he would have lived around 570 CE. The epic was translated into Anglo Saxon verse around 700 CE, and the only existing copy in the British Museum in London was made around 1000 CE. This priceless manuscript miraculously survived a fire in the eighteenth century.

The story takes place in the Kingdom of the Geats where King Hrothgar has built a splendid banqueting hall to celebrate the peace he has secured following the overthrow of his enemies.

Unknown to the King, there lurks in the fens (the surrounding marshlands) a monster called Grendel, who jealously watches the building of the hall, and plots his revenge on the humans who built it. The 'rinc' or warrior, Beowulf, overcomes the terrible monster, although this is not the end of the story, because Grendel's monster mother later comes to avenge her son's death, and Beowulf has to fight another battle.

The language is the oldest form of written English, called Old English, or Anglo-Saxon.

1 How old is the earliest surviving copy of *Beowulf*?

....

....

2 How long after the first translation into Anglo-Saxon verse of the poem was this copy made?

....

....

3 What is the present-day name for the region in which the story is set?

....

....

. . . .

. . . .

4 What two monsters does Beowulf fight against?

. . . .

. . . .

. . . .

. . . .

. . . .

. . . .

. . . .

5 Explain in your own words how *Beowulf* has come down to us.

. . . .

. . . .

. . . .

. . . .

. . . .

. . . .

Information transfer

The Tang family are planning to visit London. Chin Min Tang has visited the UK once before and is eager to show his daughters round. They have been saving up for a long time and have explored the internet to discover the best deals. Sara has been doing most of the research as she is an accomplished computer user. Like her two sisters, Suki (12) and Mai Ling (14), she is a pupil at the International School, Singapore, where she is in her final year. Her sixteenth birthday will be on 10 August and as they plan to be on holiday from 2 to 23 August, she hopes to spend it in London. While her two sisters will share, Sara has been promised a room of her own, provided the rooms are together.

They want to be somewhere in the city centre with easy access to public transport, as Sara's mother, Hong Tan, suffers from arthritis and cannot walk far, and they would like to spend up to five days of their holiday visiting a different part of the country away from the noise and rush of city life.

They have settled on a package holiday offered by Sunlight Travel Worldwide and have been sent a form to complete giving details of the family's interests and requirements.

▶ Imagine that you are Mr Tang. Complete the holiday form below.

SUNLIGHT TRAVEL WORLDWIDE – LONDON PACKAGE

Thank you for choosing Sunlight Travel Worldwide. Your satisfaction is our aim. Please complete the following so that we can arrange the best holiday to suit your requirements:

Name: ....

Number in party Adults: ....
Children: (under 5 yrs) .... (11–16 yrs) .... (16–18 yrs) ....

Is any member of your party of limited mobility? Yes / No (please delete as appropriate)

If yes, please give detail: ....

Special consideration: ....

Departure date: (please give day/month/year xx/xx/xxxx): .../.../......

Hotels participating in package: (please tick your choice)

Hotel Victoria (2 minutes walk from Victoria train and coach stations) ☐

Epsom Imperial (rural setting within short travelling distance of central London) ☐

Verulamium Spa Hotel (under 1 hour by train from central London) ☐

Room requirements: family ... double ... twin ... single ...

Special considerations: ....

5 day excursions available (1 included in package; others can be booked at extra cost)

See brochure for details

Weekend in Paris – sneak a look at our neighbours in France ☐

Sports special – play golf with a professional; visit Wembley stadium and Lords ☐

Relax in the peace and quiet of an English village ☐

Cultural tour – visit Shakespeare's birthplace, see a play, attend a concert ☐

Signed: .... **Date:** ....

Note-making

For this exercise you need to refer back to the passage *What did English look like in the past?* on page 208 in the student book, for information about Beowulf.

▶ You have been asked to give a short talk about *Beowulf* to your English class. Under the following headings make preparatory notes for your presentation.

The importance of *Beowulf*

- ....
- ....

Outline of the story

- King Hrothgar builds a banqueting hall
- ....
- ....
- ....

The language of the poem

- ....
- ....

Summary

▶ Using your notes as a basis, write a summary of *Beowulf* in not more than **50 words**.

Informal writing

The Canterbury Tales is a collection of stories imagined to have been told as a group of people travelled from London to Canterbury.

Imagine that you are on a journey. An elderly man comes and sits next to you. From the conversation you and he have, you learn that he has travelled far and wide and had many adventures, including when … and he tells you the story.

▶ Tell that story.

Writing

Today we live in a global village. More and more people are learning a second language – English perhaps – so that they can understand and be understood worldwide. Gradually we are progressing towards one common universal language.

But local languages and dialects need to be carefully preserved, too. We must not lose our linguistic identity in the process.

'Invest in a better future – learn English and conquer the world!'

'Support your local dialect and keep tradition alive!'

'Unite in one language and speak peace to all.'

'A nation's identity is best expressed in its own language. Stop local languages from dying out!'

▶ Write an article for your school magazine giving your views.

Oxford English 4

An international approach
Exam Workbook

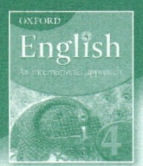

9780199126675

9780199126712

9780199116423

Oxford English: An International Approach Exam Workbook 4 for IGCSE English as a Second Language provides a wealth of prepared activities and worksheets to improve students' skills for the written tasks of the exam. These activities follow topics from the student book and use examples from the reading material to make tasks relevant and meaningful.

Activities develop skills in reading comprehension, note-making, summary writing, formal and informal writing, including essay planning and information transfer.

The Exam Workbook includes:

- Carefully stepped activities to ensure students acquire skills and achieve the best grade possible
- Clearly developed tasks based on a variety of literature types set at the appropriate level
- Suggested answers provided in Teacher's Guide 4.

OXFORD
UNIVERSITY PRESS

Great Clarendon Street, Oxford OX2 6DP

Oxford University Press is a department of the University of Oxford. It furthers the University's objective of excellence in research, scholarship, and education by publishing worldwide in

Oxford   New York

Auckland   Cape Town   Dar es Salaam   Hong Kong   Karachi
Kuala Lumpur   Madrid   Melbourne   Mexico City   Nairobi
New Delhi   Shanghai   Taipei   Toronto

With offices in

Argentina   Austria   Brazil   Chile   Czech Republic   France   Greece
Guatemala   Hungary   Italy   Japan   Poland   Portugal   Singapore
South Korea   Switzerland   Thailand   Turkey   Ukraine   Vietnam

© Oxford University Press

The moral rights of the author have been asserted

Database right Oxford University Press (maker)

First published 2010

British Library Cataloguing in Publication Data

Data available

ISBN-13: 978-0-19-912726-9

20 19 18 17

Printed in India by Multivista Global Pvt. Ltd

Paper used in the production of this book is a natural, recyclable product made from wood grown in sustainable forests. The manufacturing process conforms to the environmental regulations to the country of origin.

Cover image: Robert Harding/Getty Images

ACKNOWLEDGEMENTS

The author and publisher are grateful for permission to reprint the following copyright material:

Deborah Cadbury: extract from *The Dinosaur Hunters* (Fourth Estate, 2001), copyright © Deborah Cadbury 2001, reprinted by permission of HarperCollins Publishers Ltd.

David Crystal: extract from *Txtng: The Gr8 Db8* (OUP, 2008), in '2b or not 2b? Despite doom-laden prophesies' article published in *The Guardian Review*, 5.7.2008, reprinted by permission of Oxford University Press.

Michael Durham: 'Elephants escaping Zimbabwe damage Zambian crops and property' *The Guardian*, 28.12.2003, reprinted by permission of the author.

Fox News: 'Baghdad residents see snow for the first time', 11.1.2008, reprinted by permission of Fox News.

Anthony Horowitz: 'The Monkey Who Would be King' from *Myths and Legends* retold by Anthony Horowitz (Kingfisher, 1991), reprinted by permission of United Agents for the author.

Indira A R Lakshmanan: 'For Venezuela's Poor, Music Opens Doors', *The Boston Globe*, 22 June 2005, reprinted by permission of PARS International Inc.

Laurie Lee: extract from *Cider with Rosie* (Hogarth Press, 1959), reprinted by permission of United Agents on behalf of The Estate of Laurie Lee.

Liam O'Flaherty: 'The Sniper' originally from *Spring Sowing* (Jonathan Cape, 1926), from *Collected Short Stories* (Wolfhound Press, 1999), reprinted by permission of the publishers.

Saira Shah: extracts from *The Storyteller's Daughter: Return to a Lost Homeland* (Michael Joseph, 2003), copyright © Saira Shah 2002, reprinted by permission of Penguin Books Ltd and Random House, Inc.

Although we have made every effort to trace and contact all copyright holders before publication this has not been possible in all cases. If notified, the publisher will rectify any errors or omissions at the earliest opportunity.

OXFORD
UNIVERSITY PRESS
₹470

OXFORD
UNIVERSITY PRESS

Orders and enquiries to Customer Services:
tel. +44 (0) 1536 452620
fax +44 (0) 1865 313472

www.oxfordsecondary.co.uk

schools.enquiries.uk@oup.com

ISBN 978-0-19-912726-9

9 780199 127269